10/97

D0744548

SWAZI

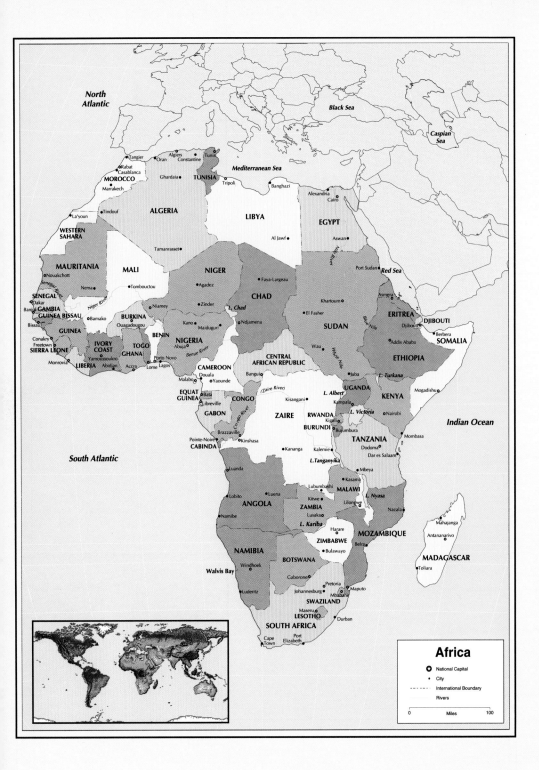

North
Atlantic

Black Sea

Caspian
Sea

Mediterranean Sea

Tangier
Algiers
Oran Constantine
Rabat
Casablanca
MOROCCO
Marrakech
Ghardaia
TUNISIA
Tripoli
Banghazi
Alexandria
Cairo

La'youn
Tindouf
ALGERIA
LIBYA
EGYPT

WESTERN
SAHARA

Al Jawf
Aswan

Tamanrasset

MAURITANIA
MALI
NIGER
CHAD
Port Sudan
Red Sea
Asmara
ERITREA
DJIBOUTI

Nouakchott
Nema
Tombouctou
Agadez
Faya-Largeau
Khartoum
Djibouti
Berbera

SENEGAL
Dakar
GAMBIA
Banjul
GUINEA BISSAU
Bissau
Niger River
Niamey
L. Chad
Zinder
Ndjamena
El Fasher
SUDAN
Addis Ababa
SOMALIA

Bamako
BURKINA
Ouagadougou
Kano
Maiduguri
Wau
ETHIOPIA

Conakry
GUINEA
BENIN
NIGERIA
White Nile
L. Turkana

Freetown
SIERRA LEONE
IVORY
COAST
TOGO
GHANA
Abuja
Benue River
CENTRAL
AFRICAN REPUBLIC
Juba
UGANDA
Mogadishu

Monrovia
LIBERIA
Yamoussoukro
Abidjan
Accra
Porto Novo
Lome
Lagos
CAMEROON
Douala
Yaounde
Bangui
(Zaire River)
L. Albert
Kisangani
Kampala
L. Victoria
KENYA
Nairobi

EQUAT.
GUINEA
Bata
Malabo
Libreville
CONGO
GABON
ZAIRE
RWANDA
Kigali
BURUNDI
Bujumbura
Mombasa

Indian Ocean

Pointe-Noire
CABINDA
Brazzaville
Kinshasa
Kananga
Kalemie
TANZANIA
Dodoma
Dar es Salaam

South Atlantic

L.Tanganyika

Luanda
Kasama
Mbeya

Lobito
Luena
Lubumbashi
MALAWI
L. Nyasa
Nacala

ANGOLA
Kitwe
ZAMBIA
Lilongwe

Namibe
Lusaka
L. Kariba
Harare
MOZAMBIQUE
Mahajanga

NAMIBIA
ZIMBABWE
Belra
Antananarivo

Walvis Bay
Windhoek
BOTSWANA
Bulawayo
MADAGASCAR

Luderitz
Gaborone
Pretoria
Maputo
Toliara

Johannesburg
Mbabane
SWAZILAND
Maseru
LESOTHO
Durban
SOUTH AFRICA

Cape
Town
Port
Elizabeth

Africa

⊗ National Capital
• City
----- International Boundary
Rivers

0 ———— Miles ———— 100

The Heritage Library of African Peoples

SWAZI

Benson O. Oluikpe, Ph.D.

THE ROSEN PUBLISHING GROUP, INC.
NEW YORK

Published in 1997 by The Rosen Publishing Group, Inc.
29 East 21st Street, New York, NY 10010

First Edition

Manufactured in the United States of America

Library of Congress Cataloging-in-Publication Data

Oluikpe, Benson Omenihu A.
    Swazi / Benson O. Oluikpe. — 1st ed.
      p.   cm. — (The heritage library of African peoples)
    Includes bibliographical references and index.
    Summary: Discusses the history, culture, and daily life of the
Swazi people of southern Africa.
    ISBN 0-8239-2012-7
    1. Swazi (African people)—Juvenile literature.   [1. Swazi
(African people)]   I. Title.   II. Series.
DT2746.S95058   1996
968′.00496398—dc20   96-32821
                                                         CIP
                                                         AC

Contents

INTRODUCTION

THERE IS EVERY REASON FOR US TO KNOW something about Africa and to understand its past and the way of life of its peoples. Africa is a rich continent that has for centuries provided the world with art, culture, labor, wealth, and natural resources. It has vast mineral deposits, fossil fuels, and commercial crops.

But perhaps most important is the fact that fossil evidence indicates that human beings originated in Africa. The earliest traces of human beings and their tools are almost two million years old. Their descendants have migrated throughout the world. To be human is to be of African descent.

The experiences of the peoples who stayed in Africa are as rich and as diverse as of those who established themselves elsewhere. This series of books describes their environment, their modes of subsistence, their relationships, and their customs and beliefs. The books present the variety of languages, histories, cultures, and religions that are to be found on the African continent. They demonstrate the historical linkages between African peoples and the way contemporary Africa has been affected by European colonial rule.

Africa is large, complex, and diverse. It encompasses an area of more than 11,700,000

square miles. The United States, Europe, and India could fit easily into it. The sheer size is an indication of the continent's great variety in geography, terrain, climate, flora, fauna, peoples, languages, and cultures.

Much of contemporary Africa has been shaped by European colonial rule, industrialization, urbanization, and the demands of a world economic system. For more than seventy years, large regions of Africa were ruled by Great Britain, France, Belgium, Portugal, and Spain. African peoples from various ethnic, linguistic, and cultural backgrounds were brought together to form colonial states.

For decades Africans struggled to gain their independence. It was not until after World War II that the colonial territories became independent African states. Today, almost all of Africa is ruled by Africans. Large numbers of Africans live in modern cities. Rural Africa is also being transformed, and yet its people still engage in many of their customs and beliefs.

Contemporary circumstances and natural events have not always been kind to ordinary Africans. Today, however, new popular social movements and technological innovations pose great promise for future development.

George C. Bond, Ph.D., Director
Institute of African Studies
Columbia University, New York

The Swazi proudly continue to follow many of their traditions. On ceremonial occasions, people often wear traditional clothing. The man above is the master of ceremonies at a wedding. He carries a Swazi club and a cowhide shield decorated with feathers. He wears a monkey apron over his cotton skirt, cowtails on his elbows, and a beaded necklace of typical Swazi design.

chapter

1

THE LAND AND THE PEOPLE

THE SWAZI PEOPLE LIVE IN A COUNTRY IN southern Africa called the Kingdom of Swaziland. Many also live in Mozambique and South Africa.

The ruling Swazi dynasty is a core group called the Ngwane. The Ngwane migrated into present-day Swaziland from the east during the mid-1700s. The Ngwane conquered and absorbed several small groups of Sotho, Tsonga, and Zulu people. As a result, these people came under Ngwane influence and gradually became the Swazi nation. Today, the Swazi have their own language and culture.

The language of the Swazi is SiSwati. English is used in business and government in Swaziland. The total number of SiSwati speakers has been estimated at almost 2 million. The population of the Kingdom of Swaziland is about 1 million, including thousands of

9

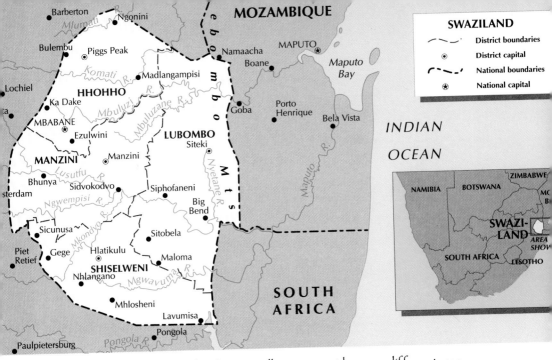

The Kingdom of Swaziland is a small country with many different geographical regions.

Europeans and persons of mixed ancestry. Most Swazi in Swaziland are farmers and raise livestock. Many live in cities such as Mbabane, the administrative capital, and work in factories, offices, and shops.

Each year thousands of Swazi go to South Africa, where they work in mining, in industries, or as domestic servants. Almost as many Swazi live in South Africa as in Swaziland. The Swazi claim that some of the land in South Africa was once Swazi territory and should be returned to the Kingdom of Swaziland.

The Kingdom of Swaziland is about the size of the state of New Jersey in the United States. Though small, it has many different environments. The country can be divided into four main geographical zones, moving from west to east.

Many Swazi live in South Africa or go there to work. In South Africa, many workers live in townships like Soweto, seen above.

The Highveld is a wide belt of rugged country in the west. The climate is cool and the rainfall is good. This area is too mountainous to support farming, but it is ideal for forestry. Swaziland has the largest commercial, planted forest in Africa, consisting of 250,000 acres of pine and eucalyptus trees.

The Middleveld has rich soil and a subtropical climate. This hilly grassland contains many

rivers, which flow strongly during the rainy season from October to March. The excellent grazing lands make the region ideal for cattle herding. Overuse of grazing land has weakened the soil, and it now washes away easily during the rainy season. This erosion has become a problem.

The Middleveld has the highest concentration of people in Swaziland. Swazi families grow food for themselves on small farms provided by the king. The most important crop is white corn. Vegetables, fruits, nuts, cotton, and tobacco are also grown. The success or failure of Swazi crops is dependent upon the annual rains.

Most of the good soil and the well-irrigated areas of the Middleveld are dominated by large agricultural estates, owned by whites. Here citrus fruits, pineapples, bananas, and rice are grown for export to other countries.

The Lowveld is hot, dry, and covered by tall grasses and tropical brush. When the rainfall is good, the grass in this area is excellent for cattle herding. Because drought is frequent in this region, Swazi farmers plant hardy crops such as sorghum (a grain), and peanuts. The Lowveld areas that are irrigated are mostly owned by white commercial farmers. They grow sugar cane, which requires a great deal of labor. Many Swazi work on these sugar plantations.

The Lubombo is a high rocky plateau that

borders Mozambique in the east of Swaziland. The Lusutfu, Mbuluzi, and Ngwavuma Rivers cut gorges in the rocky mountains. The Lubombo plateau is used for some cattle ranching and farming.

Though Swaziland is one of the best-watered countries in southern Africa, drought is a recurring problem for small-scale Swazi farmers. When the rains are good, the great rivers Ngwavuma, Nkomazi, Mbuluzi, and Lusutfu flow across the country from the Highveld toward the Indian Ocean, providing sources for irrigation and hydroelectric power.

Coal and asbestos are mined in Swaziland, and there are factories for the manufacture of cement, chocolate candy, and packing materials.

Swaziland's tourist industry includes a gambling casino in the Ezulwini Valley, and game parks in Mlilwane and Ehlane. Large wild animals are less visible today than before. But hippopotamuses, several types of antelope, lions, baboons, and monkeys are still seen on occasion. There are also crocodiles in the rivers of the Lowveld. The game parks are now stocked with the wild animals that once roamed the countryside in large numbers.▲

chapter

2

HISTORY

THE SWAZI HAVE A CULTURE, LANGUAGE,
and history similar to other groups in the region
such as the Zulu. Together these groups are
referred to as the North Nguni. As the Swazi
expanded from a few families to a small nation,
they absorbed peoples and ideas from other cultures, such as the Sotho and the Tsonga.

▼ ORIGINS OF THE NGWANE ▼

The Swazi are related to the millions of so-
called Bantu peoples who live in sub-Saharan
Africa. Many experts believe that Bantu peoples
gradually migrated into southern Africa over
many hundreds of years. However, there is a
great deal of evidence in southern Africa of very
early humans. The relationship between these
early humans and the Bantu is not yet clear.
What is clear is that many Bantu were established in southern Africa by about 500 AD.

These early Bantu societies had cattle, grain, and ironworking technology. The most important aspect of their economy was cattle. Cattle were regarded as wealth. However, these people also engaged in farming, hunting, and trade.

During the 1400s, Dlamini, the founder of the Swazi royal clan, settled with his followers near Maputo in Mozambique. The Dlamini clan remained in this area until the end of the 1700s. At this time, the name of their leader was Ngwane. Ngwane moved his people across the Lubombo mountains and settled near the bank of the Pongola River. Today the Swazi regard Ngwane as the founder of their nation, and the core clans of the Swazi nation refer to themselves as BakaNgwane, which means the people of Ngwane.

During the early 1800s, Ngwane's grandson, Sobhuza I, formed an army and began absorbing neighboring peoples. This was a period when great states rose in the region, and competition increased between them for grazing lands and control of trade routes. Cruel wars of conquest and great migrations of people occurred in this unsettled period of nation building, called the Mfecane. Sobhuza I of the Swazi, Moshoeshoe of the South Sotho or Basotho, Zwide of the Ndwandwe, and Shaka of the Zulu were all powerful leaders during the Mfecane.

Sobhuza I came into conflict with Zwide over

land. Because Zwide's Ndwandwe had a more powerful army, Sobhuza I decided to avoid war and move his people north.

As Sobhuza's people entered the western part of present-day Swaziland, they encountered other Nguni and Sotho groups. These peoples were forced to declare their loyalty to the Dlamini clan or else be destroyed. Those who accepted, and offered tribute of women and food, were allowed to keep their own chiefs and local customs. The Swazi refer to these peoples and their descendants as Emakhandzambili, which means those found ahead.

Sobhuza I increased his authority by taking herbs and medicines for war, fertility, and rain from the local chiefs. The local people believed that these medicines gave Sobhuza I supernatural power over the key elements of life. Sobhuza I also married into the families of Zwide of the Ndwandwe and Shaka of the Zulu. These marriages made Sobhuza I a relative and an ally of these powerful leaders.

When Sobhuza I died in 1839, there was a violent dispute among his people about which one of two rival princes should become the next leader of the Ngwane. Zwide's daughter, Thandile, was proclaimed queen mother and coruler of the Ngwane. Her son, Mswati, became Sobhuza's heir.

Mswati is remembered as a great fighting

CLOTHING

Swazi men and women pay much attention to their physical appearance. Except on special occasions or in remote areas of the countryside, most Swazi today wear Western clothing.

Small Swazi children traditionally wore only a band of beads or woven grass around the waist. They also wore small charms to ward off evil and sickness during their early, vulnerable years. Young men wore animal pelts around the waist. Unmarried women wore grass skirts. Once cloth began to be imported into Swazi territory, these were replaced by brightly-colored prints. Married women wore heavy skirts made of cowhide and goatskins, and kept their hair in a beehive shape. Marriageable men wore a wax "head ring" woven into their hair.

Christian missionaries frowned upon what they considered immodest Swazi clothing and encouraged the wearing of Western clothing. Today, Swazi women and men sometimes wear factory-made thin cotton cloth over their street clothes, often with wonderful patterns in red, white, and black. Swazi men and women often wear a strip of animal hide around the wrist, called *siphandla*, which protects the wearer from harm.

Hairstyles are one way that both status and beauty are displayed. Today young women may spend hours sitting together and braiding elaborate designs into each other's hair. At festivals, young men wear beautiful feathers or porcupine quills in their hair. Only the king and the royal family are permitted to wear the bright red feathers of a bird called the Knysna loerie. Some men use aloe ash to bleach their hair white, a color associated with wisdom and purity. Traditional healers and diviners roll their hair into thick strands with grease and red ocher, a kind of mineral. They dress their hair with many shells, beads, and other charms.

Many Swazi men carry a stick called a knobkerrie. Knobkerries are long clubs with an ornately carved, round knot at one end. They were once used as a weapon in battle. Now they are carried for protection when traveling and are considered a necessary sign of a gentleman.

These men in traditional dress wear feathers in their hair. The man on the right has covered his hair with an ash mixture.

king. He used the same military techniques as the Ndwandwe and the Zulu: his soldiers used short stabbing spears, and his army regiments were grouped according to age rather than clan. His raids for cattle and captives ranged far and wide, even as far north as present-day Zimbabwe.

Descendants of clans conquered by Mswati are called Emafikamuva, which means those who arrived after. Men from conquered Sotho and Nguni clans were made to serve in the Swazi army and to work the king's fields.

The name "Swazi" is an English mispronunciation of "Mswati." King Mswati is honored as the one who brought many different peoples

together to form a nation. The organization of Swazi people according to age groups and the institution of national ceremonies helped unite the various Swazi clans under Mswati. These institutions also focused the attention of the Swazi people on the king as the protector and provider of the nation.

▼ THE COMING OF THE EUROPEANS ▼

Before his death in 1839, Sobhuza I had a vision that white-skinned people would enter the country. During the time of Mswati, descendants of Dutch colonists from the Cape of Good Hope, called Boers (farmers), had begun to settle in the Transvaal region to the west of present-day Swaziland.

Meanwhile, in the south, British colonists were settling in what is now KwaZulu-Natal. The British hunted game animals, traded for ivory, and competed with the Boers for control of the region.

The Boers wanted access to a port on the Indian Ocean, but they were blocked by the British to the south and by the Swazi to the east. The Boers were also mainly cattle farmers, and they were always eager to obtain good grazing land. Boer ambitions led them to try to gain control over Swaziland.

The Swazi welcomed the first Europeans to their country in the 1840s. Although in southern

Africa, the Boers and the British competed with each other, the Swazi became allies with both. They both requested British protection from the Zulu in the south and assisted the Boers in fighting North Sotho groups to the north. In 1846 the Boers signed a treaty with an outcast Swazi leader. This treaty, without the agreement of Mswati, gave the Boers rights to most of the western Swazi lands. In 1860 Mswati granted an area in the southeast of his territory to a Boer named Vermaak. Vermaak was declared chief and was expected to provide protection from invading Zulu armies.

The Swazi king is supposed to choose a "main wife" as queen mother for his heir. At his death, Mswati had not chosen a main wife, so there was conflict for the throne. When Mswati died in 1868, the Swazi princes fought over who would be his heir as had happened when Sobhuza I died. The chosen heir was murdered by his jealous brothers. Queen Mother Sisile chose an orphan, Mbandzeni, to replace her son as king. The Boers sent a commando, or military unit, of 400 men to oversee the coronation ceremony for Mbandzeni. Increased involvement of the Boers in Swazi politics did little to calm the fighting among Swazi aristocrats.

According to Swazi custom, the king and his queen mother are supposed to rule together and balance each other's power. Mbandzeni had his

queen mother, Sisile, put to death, because she had argued with him and left the capital with her rain-making medicines.

Although the Swazi nation was disrupted by political events, the Swazi army remained as strong as ever. The British wanted to use this strength to help them crush a North Sotho people called the Pedi. The British promised to protect Swazi independence in return for military assistance. In 1880 the Swazi general Mbovana Fakudze led a heroic attack against the Pedi stronghold. The British government recognized the independence of Swaziland the following year.

At that time, gold and tin were discovered in Swaziland. Hundreds of white settlers flooded into Swaziland. They wanted rights to mine the land, herd cattle, farm, set up industries and businesses, and collect taxes.

According to Swazi tradition, royal grants of land were a means of creating alliances. The country was owned by the Swazi nation, under the leadership of their king and queen mother. Because land could not be owned by individuals, such grants were not considered permanent. White settlers chose to ignore Swazi tradition, and insisted upon their right to privately own land. Today it is unclear whether the Swazi royals intended to sell the land to the Europeans or lease it according to Swazi tradition.

In any event, almost the entire country was sold off during Mbandzeni's reign. Many Swazi people today believe that these past decisions were very much against the best interests of the Swazi nation. In their view, the whites manipulated the Swazi royalty, who allowed greed to blind them to the fact that they were losing control of their country to the British and the Dutch. Some claim that both the Swazi royalty and the white settlers "grew fat," or profited from the situation, at the expense of the common people.

In 1887 Mbandzeni created a special administration to deal with Europeans. He hired Theophilus "Offy" Shepstone, son of the British Secretary for Native Affairs in Natal, to serve as his "chief" of white residents. With the consent of the Swazi king, he formed a committee to govern and settle disputes among the white community in Swaziland. Despite the confidence placed in him by the king, Shepstone was only working to benefit himself and other whites. The influence of Offy Shepstone further weakened the control of the Swazi over their own destiny.

In some ways Mbandzeni did try to resist the economic takeover of his country by the whites. He often sold mining rights to the British for lands that had previously been given to the Boers for grazing. This kept the two settler groups in conflict with each other. But before

long most of Swaziland's valuable resources and land had been sold off to whites.

Mbandzeni died in 1889. Prince Bhunu was selected heir, but ruled only briefly. The queen mother, Gwamile, and an older prince were installed as rulers, with the responsibilities of raising the new king, Sobhuza II, and of ruling the country. Because of rivalry for the throne and the scarcity of Swazi land, a period of violence followed the death of Mbandzeni. Queen Mother Gwamile is remembered by the Swazi people for her great wisdom and moderation during a period of intense difficulty.

▼ THE LOSS OF INDEPENDENCE ▼

In 1894 the British went back on their promise of independence for Swaziland. Against the wishes of the Swazi, they handed Swaziland over to the Boers' Transvaal Republic as a protectorate, that is, a territory that is taken over by a more powerful state under the guise of protecting it. In fact, the "protected" country is often exploited by its "protector."

This was a period of terrible distress for the Swazi people. Rinderpest, a cattle disease, swept through the Swazi herds, destroying the Swazi's most cherished source of wealth. The Boer government imposed taxes on the people, which had to be paid in cash. Combined these two problems crushed the economy of the Swazi

The Swazi system of government and many of their traditions were changed by the arrival of whites. In the picture above, a chief (on the far left) oversees the present-giving ceremony at an engagement.

farmers. The Swazi people had formerly been able to take care of themselves by raising crops and keeping cattle. Now they were forced to work for white owners of farms and industries at very low pay in order to obtain cash to pay taxes. Many Swazi men went to the gold mines in South Africa as laborers.

The Boers were defeated by the British in the Anglo-Boer War. In 1902 the British took control of the government of Swaziland, which now became a British protectorate. The British continued the taxation policy of the Boers, and they brought in Zulu police to enforce tax collection.

The Swazi hoped that the British protectorate

An important resource in rural Swaziland is grass for thatched roofs. This woman, wearing the traditional hairstyle of married women, is cutting grass.

government would give them back their land that had been taken by settlers. But the needs of the settlers and the British Empire came first. In 1907 a British land commission divided up Swaziland into "white areas" and "native areas." The Swazi living in the newly-defined white areas were forced to move into the "native areas," which made up only about one-third of the country. The land reserved for the Swazi was often the territory with the poorest soil and fewest resources. Also, the British kept the right to develop mining industries in the African reserve areas. The development of roads, irrigation, and communications in white

areas was paid for by Swazi "native taxes."

The British, like the Boers, hoped that their taxation and land policies would force the Swazi to abandon herding and farming, and become cheap workers for the whites. Some Swazi had no choice but to work on white farms for no pay, receiving in return only a place to live and some food. To this day, the economy and future prospects of Swaziland are largely tied to business interests and political conditions in South Africa.

In their governing of Swaziland, the British followed the formula of "indirect rule," which they used in many other parts of their empire. Under this scheme, the British controlled the people they colonized by using the institutions already set up in the country. The British left the traditional Swazi councils and courts in place, but gave final say in all "native affairs" to the British Commissioner in Swaziland. The Swazi royal heir during most of this period, Sobhuza II, was forbidden to call himself "king." All the affairs of the whites in Swaziland were handled by a separate court that followed British law. Africans could appeal to the British courts if they were not satisfied with a ruling in their traditional courts.

▼ RESISTANCE, THE ROYALTY, ▼ AND INDEPENDENCE

Queen Mother Gwamile realized that the only

King Sobhuza II, seen here, led his country to independence. He died in 1982 and was succeeded by King Mswati III.

way to combat British control was to fight them on their own terms. She saw that money and literacy were the keys to power in the Western world. She was determined that the young king, Sobhuza II, would be rich and well-educated. She established a small school for princes and nobles in Swaziland. For his college education, Sobhuza II was sent to Lovedale College in South Africa.

When the Swazi were given the right to collect taxes, Gwamile used this money to pay for the education of the king, to cure the cattle disease, and to buy back land for the Swazi nation. She also helped fund the African National Congress (ANC) in South Africa, which was formed to promote the rights of black people in southern Africa. Today South Africa has become a democratic country ruled by the ANC.

After being installed as king in 1921, Sobhuza II fought to regain land through the British courts and established the Lifa Fund to buy back land for the native people.

When independence was granted to Swaziland in 1968, more than half of the country was again owned by the Swazi nation, and the power of the royal Dlamini family had been greatly increased.▲

chapter

3

SOCIETY AND CULTURE

TODAY MANY SWAZI LIVE IN BIG CITIES IN southern Africa and other parts of the world, where their lifestyle is similar to that of other city dwellers. It is mostly in rural Swaziland that many Swazi continue to practice the customs of their traditional way of life. Wherever they may be, most Swazi are proud of their cultural heritage. National holidays give Swazi people a way to celebrate and remember their heritage.

▼ THE SWAZI HOMESTEAD ▼

Rural Swazi villages are made up of a group of homesteads, called *umuti*. An individual house within the homestead is called an *indlu*.

The traditional house of Nguni peoples, including the early Swazi or Ngwane, is a beehive-shaped house. Seldom seen today, these houses have wooden frames covered with many different kinds of grass that are woven together.

Early beehive houses had low arched doorways that had to be crawled through in order to enter. Designed to protect the dwellers against animals and intruders, the low threshold is not as important today. Houses are arranged in a semi-circle around a central cattle pen.

Another kind of house seen in rural areas and favored by other southern African peoples is the *rondavel*. It has a cone-shaped thatched roof placed on a circular wall. The wall is made of

The traditional Swazi house seen here has a beehive shape and an expertly woven grass covering. Such houses are seldom seen today. Many Swazi now live in Western-style houses.

Polygyny, the practice of having more than one wife, is allowed under Swazi customary law. This occurs less frequently today than in the past. Each wife has her own house or houses in the homestead. Part of a rural wife's daily work is to grind grain for meals, as the woman above is doing.

packed earth and grass. Floors are generally made of hard, flattened earth, and polished to a smooth shine. Cooking may be done in the center of the house or in the courtyard.

In the past, homes contained little furniture. Woven mats were used for sitting and sleeping, and a carved wooden headrest served as a pillow. Today rural houses generally contain store-bought furnishings.

More than one style of house may be found in the same rural homestead. Newer types include Western-style, rectangular homes made of earth or cement brick, with a roof of thatched

31

Today many Swazi live in cities and use modern appliances. However, in rural areas, women wash their family's clothes in a nearby river.

grass or corrugated iron. Houses and communities in the cities are similar to those in the Western world.

A traditional, rural homestead is the residence of a man and his wives, their small children, married sons, and unmarried daughters. Swazi men are allowed to have several wives, provided they can afford to support them. If a man has more than one wife, each wife is entitled to two or more houses that have a living room, a store room, and a kitchen. In addition, each wife owns one or more small structures that hold grain. Older boys, girls, and family guests stay in separate houses. Each wife controls her own living areas, raises her children, and cultivates her own gardens.

Today many rural women sell items they produce in nearby markets. This woman's baskets might be bought by locals or visitors.

Outside the homestead, family gardens are arranged across the landscape. Here women and children spend most of their time weeding, planting, and harvesting vegetables. Beyond the gardens are the grazing lands where the boys tend the family cattle.

For the men, the cattle pen, or *sibaya*, is the center of traditional village life. The *sibaya* is a wide, circular enclosure made of stacked brushwood or closely packed wooden poles. The entrance to the *sibaya* faces away from the homestead. The *sibaya* is the men's meeting place. Here they spend their leisure time, settle village disputes, and receive visitors. Women are only allowed to enter on special occasions. The

33

best grain from the fields is stored in deep pits dug in the *sibaya*. When the male head of the homestead, or *umnumzana*, dies, he is buried at the entrance of the cattle pen.

Houses are arranged around the *sibaya*. The headman's mother lives in the "great house," or *indlunkulu*. She is considered a wise and powerful member of the family. Her house contains the family shrine, where the headman offers beer and meat to honor his ancestors and to bless the family. Traditionally the great house was used as the headquarters of the headman. Today many headmen have their own separate living quarters.

The country is divided into districts of several thousand people. Chiefs supervise the homesteads of each district and are either chosen by their community or appointed by the king. Districts are divided into smaller units, each under the authority of an official called an *indvuna* (plural: *tindvuna*). Chiefs and *tindvuna* meet together periodically to discuss important events, decide court cases, and suggest policy for the Swazi nation.

▼ NDLOVUKAZI AND NGWENYAMA ▼

The rulers of the Swazi state are the queen mother and her son, the king. She is called Ndlovukazi, the lady elephant, and he is called Ngwenyama, the lion. Together they rule the government and religious life of the Kingdom of

Swaziland. A royal council, called *liqoqo*, and the *libandla*, a national council that represents all the men of Swaziland, recommend policy to the king. But final decisions of state are made by the king and queen mother.

The king is the chief executive and the religious and ceremonial leader of the state. His power, though, comes from his mother. This is because it is her status as the former king's wife and as his mother that determined his selection as king. Harmony between them is necessary for peace in the nation. The queen mother offers advice, and even criticism, to the king. Together they control the sacred medicines that bring rain to the land.

They live in separate capitals in the countryside. The queen mother's homestead is considered the main capital of the Swazi nation. Though the king is in charge of the highest court, persons seeking protection are offered safety at the homestead of the Ndlovukazi. It is at her residence, the *indlunkulu*, that the king honors the spirits of past kings. This ritual ensures that they will bring prosperity to the Swazi.

In areas not owned by whites, the king is the sole owner of all property. The land and cattle of the country are all officially entrusted to the king by the Swazi nation. He distributes this property among the various princes and

chiefs, who in turn distribute the land out to *tindvuna*, or district officials.

▼ THE CYCLE OF LIFE ▼

The Swazi separate the life of a person into several different stages, each with its own set of ceremonies. Today some Christian Swazi and those in cities do not follow these customs.

In traditional Swazi culture, a baby is considered a "thing" and is not given a name for three months. After this period, it is introduced to the world in a ceremony where the child is held out to the moon and given a name. At about three years of age, the baby is weaned and left in the care of its grandparents and siblings, who teach the child songs, dances, and riddles.

At about age six, Swazi children are given a small cut in the lobe of each ear. They are expected to accept this painful experience with bravery. From then on, they are taught to control their emotions in public. In rural areas, the boys go off together to herd cattle, while the girls stay at the homestead and help their mothers fetch water and wood, cook meals, and work in the vegetable gardens.

The next stage is puberty, which, although important, has no special initiation ceremonies. During this period, young men between the ages of seventeen and twenty-seven and women between fifteen and seventeen are encouraged to

Along with their normal duties, including going to school, young Swazi boys learn how to herd animals and perform traditional dances. These boys wear costumes made from leaves.

develop relationships and explore their sexuality.

The Swazi royal family uses the puberty stage as a way of bringing the nation together. Young Swazi girls take part in the annual ceremony called Umhlanga. Boys are grouped into regiments organized according to age. These practices serve to focus attention on the king and queen mother, the centers of the Swazi nation.

▼ UMHLANGA ▼

Each year in July or August, young, unmarried Swazi girls travel to the queen mother's capital for the Umhlanga ceremony. The girls, wearing only short skirts, beads, and tassels of colored yarn, cut long reeds from the river and carry them to the queen mother's house. The word *umhlanga* means reed, so the ceremony is

An annual Swazi event is the Umhlanga, or reed ceremony, seen here. Unmarried girls in traditional costumes carry long reeds to the queen mother's house. There they repair the reed fence around her homestead.

named after the reeds. The reeds are used to repair the high screen that surrounds the queen's *indlunkulu*. Afterward, the girls perform dances and songs in honor of the Ndlovukazi. This allows them to show off their physical charms to the royal family and other onlookers.

Some educated and Christian Swazi women

object to this ceremony as a kind of "marriage market." In the past, the king could choose to marry any of the unwed women who appealed to him at the ceremony. Today many feel that young Swazi women should be focusing on their education and career rather than following the former tradition of early marriage. For others it is seen as a celebration of the beauty of the nation's women.

▼ AGE REGIMENTS ▼

All Swazi men are grouped according to age into a regiment, or *libutfo*. The men in this regiment or group remain close throughout their lives. Approximately every five years the king declares the creation of a new *libutfo*. At this time the previous *libutfo* is allowed to marry. Age-mates are gathered together in companies, led by royal princes.

Men of the same age group and regiment develop strong emotional ties. This unites men from all areas of the country, regardless of their loyalty to particular family groups and local chiefs. The *libutfo* also creates a link between all Swazi men and their king.

Until the 1900s the *libutfo* was the source of warriors for the military. During times of great national need, the king would delay the creation of a new age regiment. This prevented the older men from marrying and brought in younger

Male dancers play an important role at national celebrations. Several dances recall the strong warrior traditions of the past; others express modern-day experiences, such as working in the mines.

members so that the national workforce and army would continue to grow.

Today, as before, the youngest *libutfo* is used as a labor force in the royal homesteads and fields. Work teams begin and end the day by singing and dancing the *hlehla* in the cattle pen. In the *hlehla* dance, workers both dance as a group and give solo performances, praising their own achievements.

The *hlehla* and other regimental dances and songs have been adapted by those who travel to South Africa to work in the mines. They include details in their songs about their long journeys to the mines and the dangers and adventures of mine work.

▼ MARRIAGE ▼

Although today Swazi couples generally marry for love, in the past, they married to create alliances between families. The Swazi practice polygyny, which means that a man may have more than one wife. Women are only allowed one husband. In the past, multiple marriages created alliances with several families and enabled a man to build a large family, which provided labor for his homestead.

Today only a few wealthy older men have many wives. This is because the family of each wife must be given *lobola*, which is usually a gift of cattle. Today expensive gifts are sometimes given instead of cattle. King Sobhuza II had sixty-five wives.

Today some educated and Christian Swazi consider giving payment for a wife to be degrading. Still, many educated women demand at least a small *lobola* as a symbol of future security. Traditional Swazi regard *lobola* as insurance that the woman and her children will be cared for by her new family.

TRADITIONAL MARRIAGE

A traditional Swazi marriage is an elaborate public ceremony that acts out the past and future relationship between two families.

The bride's mother cries and instructs her daughter to observe proper codes of conduct at the groom's home. Her father prays for her protection while she lives at the in-laws' home. The bride then sets out for the groom's home with close friends, brothers, and family elders. Her parents remain behind.

The wedding party arrives at the in-laws' dressed in their finest clothes and beads. The bride is covered with blankets and wears a cloth veil over her face. Attached to the veil is the gallbladder, filled with air, of the goat that has been sacrificed to bring her good fortune in her marriage. The shape of the gallbladder suggests the swollen belly of a pregnant woman while the air is a symbol of "the breath of life."

When the groom's family greets them, the bride neither smiles nor takes notice. Later, she stands in her husband's cattle pen and sings a sad song about the loss of her freedom. Her brothers then rush in and pretend to rescue her, but she returns when her mother-in-law promises her the gift of a cow.

As a symbol of the loss of her virginity, the bride is covered with red ocher, and a small child is placed in her lap. The marriage feast lasts for several days, during which the groom's family slaughters an ox for both families to share.

At the birth of her first child, a young wife is finally considered a woman. At this point she is also more fully a part of her husband's family, because she has increased the family by providing a new child.

Here, a bride, dressed in a blanket and a veil, walks to her groom's homestead (top). She is accompanied by female relatives. A younger sister leads the party, carrying the bride's sleeping mat, headrest, and a knife to symbolize her virginity. The most important part of the ceremony is when the bride enters the cattle pen of her groom's family (middle). The groom's mother, holding a grass broom, leads her female relatives in a welcoming dance (bottom).

An example of how *lobola* strengthens ties between families is the marriage of a man to a woman from his father's mother's family. The Swazi consider this sort of marriage ideal, for the families can confirm the original alliance made by the grandparents.

The family of a bride often keeps the *lobola* cattle they have received from her marriage to use later as *lobola* payments for her brothers' brides. Because of this, brothers and sisters are traditionally considered "cattle-linked," since the brother would be unable to create a family of his own without the cattle acquired through his sister's marriage. When a married woman visits her brother and his family, she is therefore treated with great respect. The brother's children are told to honor her as a "female father."

The father is considered the head of the homestead. The mother controls the affairs and property of her *indlu*, or household. Property is inherited from father to son, since it is the son who must, in later years, provide a home for his own wives and children.

Though children are given their father's clan name, the importance of the mother in the family is significant. The father's mother's house is considered the spiritual center for the family. It is from her family that wives are sought for the men of the homestead. When a Swazi king

dies, power normally shifts to the queen mother until a new king is chosen.

▼ OLD AGE ▼

Older members of the community are highly respected by the Swazi. Life experiences are believed to provide a deep education. Also, old men and women are said to be living on the edge of the sacred world of the ancestor spirits.

Elders were once the leaders of all religious practices that connected a family to its ancestors. They were the primary educators of the young. Grandparents and grandchildren have traditionally developed a very close relationship. However, the influence of Western education and industrialization has lessened the role of the elderly in Swazi society.▲

chapter

4

THE SPIRITUAL WORLD

SWAZI BELIEVE IN A CREATOR CALLED Mvelimqanti, which means the first to appear. Mvelimqanti has had little to do with the lives of humans since the first days of creation. Mvelimqanti first brought death, which is represented by the lizard, into the world.

When a person dies, the Swazi believe that all aspects of a person's character and spirit leave the body and take up residence in the spirit world beneath the ground. The spirit becomes an ancestor, or *lidloti*, and lives in a society that mirrors the world of the living.

The relationship between humans and ancestors is the basis of traditional Swazi religion. The male head of the family and his mother appeal to the ancestors in cases of illness and economic misfortune. It is believed that the ancestors punish the living when they do not uphold their legal and moral duties.

The spirits of dead mothers and fathers guide and protect their children throughout life. The Swazi people offer meat and beer to their ancestors to ensure the well-being of the homestead. At every meal, a little food is set aside to thank the ancestors. Before drinking home-brewed beer or sour milk, some is poured onto the earth, inviting the ancestors to share.

The ancestors of the royal family guide and protect the entire nation. The king and queen mother look to the spirits of the Dlamini clan to protect the Swazi people and their land.

In Swazi homesteads, a special ox is set aside to honor and commemorate the family ancestors. This ox may not be abused or killed. So too the king keeps a sacred herd of cattle, given by his people, that honors both the ancestors of the king and the nation.

The spine of a dead person is thought to turn into a snake. If a snake enters the house, it is left alone, because it is said that a *lidloti* is visiting. Ancestors of the royal Dlamini clan manifest as deadly black mamba snakes.

Today many Swazi identify themselves as Christian. However, like most of the ethnic groups of southern Africa, the Swazi combine traditional and Western elements into their religious practice. Most Swazi continue to worship their ancestors while also being members of Christian churches. This does not conflict with their Christian beliefs.

▼ TRADITIONAL HEALERS ▼

The Swazi have two kinds of healers: *tinyanga* (singular: *inyanga*) and *tangoma* (singular: *sangoma*). *Tinyanga* are specialists in herbal medicine, while *tangoma* are diviners or seers. The king is regarded as having the most powerful medicines and divination ability in the land.

Knowledge of religious rituals and medicines is passed from father to son by *tinyanga*. *Tinyanga* work with homeopathic remedies. Many of these plant remedies have proven useful in fighting illnesses. Patients often travel long distances to visit highly recognized *tinyanga*. *Tinyanga* are usually, but not always, men.

Tangoma, who are often women, are considered more powerful than *tinyanga*. Spirits are said to select a person to become a *sangoma* by possessing them with a mysterious illness. Possession by a family spirit means that one has a special connection to the spirit world. Such persons are encouraged to become diviners. Physical and emotional pain that cannot be easily cured are signs of possession.

The period of training for a novice, or trainee, *sangoma* is long and difficult. During this time the novice walks through the land in a dream state, unable to sleep or eat. Special medicines enable her to hear the spirits more clearly. At the end of the training, *tangoma* have a public graduation ceremony, at which members of the

Tinyanga are herbalists who specialize in making medicines from plants and animal parts. *Tangoma* (top left and bottom) are diviners who work closely with spiritual forces. Today both kinds of traditional doctors often purchase supplies from a medicine store (top right). This is because some items, such as the monkey carcass in the picture, are not easily obtained in the wild.

community hide certain items. The *tangoma* are expected to prove their powers by finding the hidden objects using their enhanced "smelling" skills.

Tangoma, like psychologists, have a keen understanding of human nature. Since the Swazi believe that every disease or misfortune has a social cause, it is up to the *sangoma* to determine what has gone wrong in a sick person's human relationships.

After smoking a powerful drug called *insangu*, the diviner dances into a trance and is possessed by the spirits. She then makes a series of statements to her client. The client's responses help her to determine the nature and source of the problem. The *sangoma* then offers advice for a cure based on this knowledge. *Tangoma* exorcise, or draw out, evil spirits and often send their clients to an *inyanga*, or herbal doctor, for medicines.

The greatest enemies of Swazi society are called *batsakatsi*, or witches. These are persons believed to use spiritual medicines to carry out evil deeds. *Batsakatsi* are said to work secretly at night and to use human body parts in their medicines. *Tangoma* and *tinyanga* are often called upon to rid society of the *batsakatsi*.

Because misfortune for the Swazi is usually linked to a social cause, accusations of witchcraft increase greatly during times of human suffering. During the difficult economic period of the

1970s and early 1980s, many people were accused of witchcraft. The number of murders of suspected witches in Swaziland rose dramatically.

▼ CHRISTIANS AND SEPARATISTS ▼

Christian missionaries have been welcomed in Swaziland for over 150 years. They started some of the first schools and hospitals. Today about 60 percent of Swazi call themselves Christian. Members of churches often reject what they consider to be "backward" beliefs and customs, particularly traditional dress and polygyny. However, most Christians in Swaziland remain loyal to the royal family, visit traditional healers, and honor their ancestors.

Since the 1930s, an increasing number of Swazi have converted to independent, Africanist churches. These churches, often headed by popular leaders, combine Christian ideas and traditional African customs. Prophets in these churches may become possessed, like *tangoma*, and practice divination and exorcism through the Christian Holy Ghost.

More women than men have converted to Christianity in Swaziland. Many women have found that the churches give them new possibilities for expressing themselves. Some welcome the freedom from the strict traditional rules regarding the ancestors, polygyny, and *lobola*. Some churches encourage women to play more important roles in society, as equals of men.▲

The larger towns in Swaziland have modern buildings and facilities, such as malls and government buildings. Pictured on the left is a view of downtown Mbabane, the capital of Swaziland. In rural areas women buy supplies from small stores, such as the one below.

Like many African countries, Swaziland has a mix of urban (top) and rural (right) lifestyles, blending both traditional and contemporary elements. The fact that Swazi women are now playing an increasingly important role in government is one example of how traditions continually adapt to new circumstances.

5

SWAZILAND AFTER INDEPENDENCE

THE KINGDOM OF SWAZILAND WAS GRANTED independence from Britain in 1968. The government of the new country was a constitutional monarchy, based on the British system. But the Swazi king and his royal advisory council have more power than in the British system.

Since independence, events in Swaziland have been greatly influenced by competition between three groups: the Swazi royalty, the educated African elite, and the white population. White individuals and white-owned companies control a great deal of the best Swazi land and mines. The economy of Swaziland is heavily dependent upon the economy of South Africa. Its unit of money, the Lilangeni, is fixed to the value of the South African Rand. Swazi workers in the South African mines send their wages home, and so contribute a large percentage of the income of rural families in Swaziland.

The king controls Swazi Nation Lands, which cover more than half the country. Some of this land is parceled out to local chiefs in exchange for their loyalty. The rest of the land, including the industrial projects developed there, is controlled independently by the king through the Tibiyo Taka Ngwane Fund. Tibiyo is the largest company in Swaziland; it operates tax-free and independent of government supervision. The heads of Tibiyo are some of the most powerful men in Swaziland.

Since the colonial period, growing numbers of educated Africans have become teachers, businessmen, and government officials. Over the past thirty years, this educated elite has begun to speak for the interests of Swazi farmers and workers who were once controlled by the monarchy.

▼ PARLIAMENTARY CRISES ▼

Government land policies during the 1970s transferred more valuable property into the hands of the African elite and the royal family. The majority of Swazi, however, had poor living conditions and limited access to land. Many people crowded into the cities in search of work. Protests for better working conditions by industrial workers and farm laborers were stopped by company-paid *tindvuna*, or district officials.

In 1973 candidates who supported labor unions were elected to Parliament. The royal

family saw this as a threat to its authority, so King Sobhuza II abolished the constitution, banned all political parties, and ruled the country by decree. He appointed a committee to write a new constitution that would be more in line with Swazi traditions as he saw them, that is, one that gave him great control.

In 1977 a strike by school teachers demanding higher pay was supported by thousands of students. Mass riots in the cities of Mbabane and Manzini were broken up violently by police. The public reacted strongly against these events and bitterly criticized the king's policy.

The king put a new constitution in place in 1978. It allowed local councils to nominate candidates for Parliament, whom the king could approve or reject. The king could appoint his own candidates, but they were limited to suggesting policies. Critics pointed out that the local councils were mostly based in rural areas where the people were supportive of the royalty. Urban and industrial areas, where workers rights were at issue, were poorly represented in the new parliament.

▼ DEATH OF SOBHUZA II ▼

King Sobhuza II reigned for sixty years. When he died in 1982, he was one of the world's oldest reigning monarchs. He is remembered for peacefully leading the Swazi nation to

independence. Queen Dzeliwe was named queen mother, and her fifteen-year-old son, Prince Makhosetive, was the heir to the throne. Queen Mother Dzeliwe was to lead the nation while the young prince prepared for his future role as king.

The period following the death of Sobhuza II, like earlier periods of Swazi succession, was characterized by violence between members of the royal family. Queen Dzeliwe was sent into exile. Her sister was appointed queen mother by the *liqoqo*, the traditional royal council.

▼ A NEW KING ▼

Prince Makhosetive was named King Mswati III on April 25, 1986. Within a month he had disbanded the *liqoqo* and accused several of its members of treason. He made parliamentary elections more democratic, but important decisions are still made by the king and a small group of elders and advisors.

Despite its size, Swaziland receives a great deal of foreign aid. Critics claim that foreign aid has been spent on development projects that help a few Swazi, but neglect the needs of the urban and rural poor. Access to clean water and proper diet are problems for many Swazi. The economy of Swaziland, though, has fared much better in recent decades than that of many other African countries.▲

6

NCWALA, FESTIVAL OF FIRST FRUITS

EACH YEAR AT HARVEST TIME THE SWAZI
people celebrate Ncwala, a royal ceremony that
renews the king's personal and spiritual strength.
The tradition is seen by many Swazi as a celebration of national and cultural unity. Ncwala
symbolizes Swazi ideas about history, kingship,
fertility of the land, rebellion, and military
strength. All Swazi have a role to play in
Ncwala. As a king grows older, the importance
of Ncwala increases.

Ncwala takes place in the *sibaya,* or cattle
pen, at the queen mother's capital shortly after
the first harvest of the farming year. It begins in
December, during the new moon. Outsiders are
barred from the capital during this time. Ritual
specialists go to the Indian Ocean and to the
main rivers of the country to collect water and
medicines to give the king spiritual power.

There are two main phases of Ncwala. At the
opening of the first phase, called the Small

The most important event of the year in Swaziland is the Ncwala ceremony, which celebrates the power of the king. Seen above is an assembly of Swazi regiments, in both traditional and contemporary uniforms. Below, a crowd of women spectators includes many women from the royal family, who wear red feathers in their hair to show their status.

Ncwala, the oldest age regiment dances in a crescent moon formation and sings praises to the king. Other participants, dressed in wild animal skins and rare feathers, join the sacred celebration by singing and dancing along.

The high point of the ceremony occurs when the dancers move into a circle that represents the full moon. Suddenly the people are called to silence. Then the king spits powerful medicine to the east and to the west. The crowd shouts, "He stabs it!", indicating that the king has "killed" the old year and has renewed the fertility of the earth for the new year. This ritual is repeated at dawn.

The people go back to their homes, and come back to the *sibaya* at full moon. The people sing songs that insult the king as they prepare elaborate costumes for the next phase. The Small Ncwala symbolically separates the king from his people so that he can then move on to the next phase of the ceremony, called the Great Ncwala.

The Great Ncwala involves rituals that are intended to enhance the king's fertility. Young men cut tree branches under the light of the full moon while chanting soothing songs. For two days the people gather the cut branches. On the second day, these branches are used to cover the king's ritual house called the *inhlambelo*, in the center of the *sibaya*.

On the third day, the king strikes a black bull with a special stick that contains medicine for

fertility. Young men strip off their costumes, chase the bull, and beat it with their fists. The bull is dragged back to the *inhlambelo*, where it is sacrificed to the royal ancestors. Then the sacred ox that represents the king's ancestors in the royal herd is driven into the *sibaya* and forced to its knees. The king approaches the ox naked and sits upon its back. He sits as the "bull of the people" symbolic of national strength, and is bathed with powerful medicines. At night the king again spits medicines to strengthen the land, while the warriors dance and sing in the circle of the full moon.

The height of the Ncwala comes when the king appears to the crowd in a fierce costume of black medicines, wild grasses, and animal skins. Royal princes are asked to leave the *sibaya*, and the king dances with his loyal followers. Finally, the king tosses a green gourd onto the shield of an age-mate, symbolizing the end of the old year and the start of the new, with his power restored.

Over the next two days the people remain quiet, refraining from washing or merry-making. During this period, they burn ceremonial items from the Ncwala. The king walks naked around the fire, sprinkling sacred water. At the end of the ceremony, people sing songs and expect rain to fall, drenching them and putting out their fire. The people then can return to their homes and finally eat the fruits of the new season.▲

Glossary

Boer Settler of Dutch, or Afrikaner, origin.

elite A group with power or influence due to rank or education.

exorcise To get rid of an evil spirit.

indlu Wife's household.

indlunkulu The great house of a homestead; the residence of the headman's mother.

indvuna (**plural:** *tindvuna*) District official.

libutfo Regiment; division of Swazi men according to age.

lidloti Spirit of an ancestor.

lobola Gifts given to the family of a bride.

Mfecane An unsettled period of nation building.

Ncwala Royal ceremony of fertility and strength.

Ndlovukazi Queen mother.

Ngwenyama King.

parliament Council that is the highest law-making body of certain countries.

polygyny Practice of having more than one wife.

sibaya Cattle pen; the traditional center of village life.

tangoma (**singular:** *sangoma*) Diviners.

tinyanga (**singular:** *inyanga*) Specialists in herbal medicine.

tribute A payment by one person or nation to another as an act of submission or for protection.

Umhlanga Ceremony for adolescent girls.

umnumzana Male head of a homestead.

For Further Reading

Kuper, H. "Ncwala in Swaziland." *African Arts*, Vol. 1, No. 3, Spring, 1968.

Matsebula, J. S. M. *A History of Swaziland*. Cape Town, South Africa: Longman, 1976.

Wentzel, Volkmar. "Swaziland Tries Independence." *National Geographic*, Vol. 136, Vol. 2, August, 1969.

West, Maretin, and Jean Morris. *Abantu: An Introduction to the Black People of South Africa*. Cape Town, South Africa: Struik, 1976.

Challenging Reading

Booth, Alan R. *Swaziland: Tradition and Change in a Southern African Kingdom*. Boulder, CO: Westview Press, 1983.

Kuper, Hilda. *The Swazi: A South African Kingdom*. New York: Holt, Reinhart and Winston, 1986.

Malan, J. S. *Swazi Culture*. Pretoria, South Africa: Africa Institute of South Africa, 1985.

Index

ACKNOWLEDGMENTS
The publisher would very much like to thank John Peffer, who is currently writing his dissertation on a southern African topic for the Department of Art History and Archeology at Columbia University in New York City, for his research and assistance on this project.

ABOUT THE AUTHOR
Dean of the Faculty of Arts at the University of Nigeria, Nsukka, Dr. Benson O. Oluikpe is a professor of Applied Linguistics in the Department of Linguistics and Nigerian Languages. Professor Oluikpe's work has been published in academic journals. He specializes in writing English course books at all levels for the Nigerian educational system.

PHOTO CREDITS All photos by Jean Morris, except p. 27 and p. 52 (top), courtesy of Elizabeth A. Schneider.

CONSULTING EDITOR Gary N. van Wyk, Ph.D.

LAYOUT AND DESIGN Kim Sonsky